MIND OVER MISERY:

UNLOCKING THE POWER OF THOUGHT TO TRANSFORM SUFFERING

How Changing Your Thoughts Can Reduce Pain and Lead to Emotional Healing

Adrienne Morris

Contents

Introduction

You can't connect the dots looking forward; you can only connect them looking backwards. So you have to trust that the dots will somehow connect in your future.

–Steve Jobs

Have you ever felt like your life was a jigsaw puzzle with missing pieces, a story with chapters that just didn't seem to fit together? I have. I've spent countless nights wrestling with questions like, "Why me? Why this pain? Why does life feel so damn hard?" It's easy to feel lost and alone in these moments, to believe that the struggles we face are just random, meaningless events. But what if I told you there's a hidden pattern, a deeper meaning woven into the fabric of our experiences?

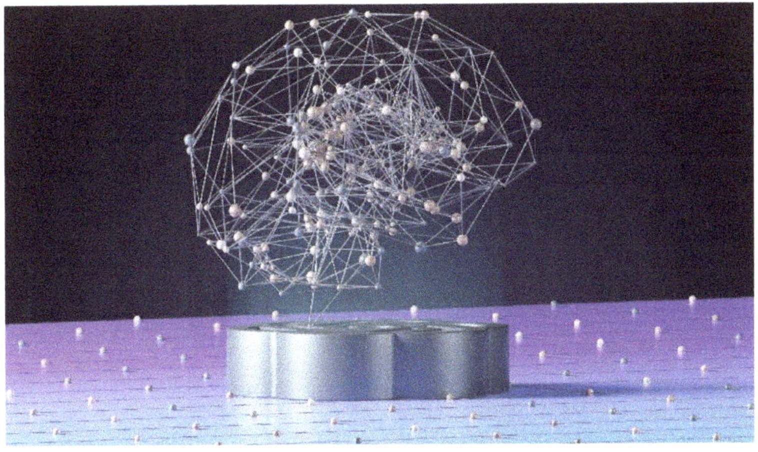

This book isn't merely another self-help guide loaded with empty promises. It's a raw, honest account of my own journey through the trenches of chronic pain, emotional trauma, and the relentless grip of negative thoughts. It's a story of resilience, of finding hope in the darkest corners, and of discovering that even the most painful experiences can become catalysts for profound transformation.

I've learned that the key to unlocking a life of joy, resilience, and healing lies not in avoiding or denying our pain, but in embracing it, understanding it, and using it as fuel for our growth. It's about recognizing that every experience, no matter how difficult, has something to teach us, something to contribute to the tapestry of our lives.

In the pages that follow, we'll explore the fascinating world of neuroscience, uncovering the intricate dance between our minds and bodies. We'll see how our thoughts, emotions, and beliefs can literally shape our physical health, and how we can harness this power to heal ourselves from the inside out.

We'll also delve into the depths of the subconscious mind, that vast reservoir of memories and beliefs that often operates beneath our conscious awareness. We'll learn how to rewrite the outdated scripts that no longer serve us, replacing limiting beliefs with empowering truths that can propel us toward our dreams.

But this journey isn't just about rewiring our brains; it's about awakening to the full spectrum of our human experience. We'll explore the transformative power of mindfulness, the healing potential of forgiveness, and the importance of nurturing positive relationships and pursuing our passions.

This book is not a magic wand; it won't erase all of your problems overnight. But it will offer you a compass, a map to guide you on your own unique journey toward healing and wholeness. It will empower you to take charge of your thoughts, your emotions, and your life, creating a reality that reflects your true potential.

So, if you're ready to embark on this adventure, to connect the dots of your own life and create a future that's brighter than you ever imagined possible, I invite you to turn the page and begin. Remember, even the longest and most challenging journey begins with a single, courageous step. And as you take that first step, trust that you're not alone. We're all in this together, learning, growing, and evolving as we navigate the beautiful messiness of life.

Chapter 1

Your Thoughts Are Leading to Your Pain

Have you ever noticed a knot tightening in your stomach as you anticipate a difficult conversation? Or felt a headache creeping in after a day filled with stress and frustration? Perhaps your shoulders ache with the weight of worry, or your back throbs with the burden of past hurts. These aren't random occurrences; they're powerful signals from your body, a language whispering the undeniable truth that your thoughts and emotions aren't confined to your mind. They profoundly affect your physical health.

In this chapter, we'll explore the mechanisms by which our thoughts influence our bodies. We'll delve into the intricate dance between mind and body, uncovering how fleeting worries and persistent anxieties can trigger a cascade of physiological responses. But this isn't merely a scientific exploration. We'll also illuminate the profound ways in which our thoughts shape our lives, from childhood experiences that leave lasting imprints on our emotional landscape to the power of mindfulness in cultivating present-moment awareness.

Together, we'll uncover the hidden forces that shape our well-being, paving the way for a life of greater peace, joy, and resilience.

The Neuroscience Behind Thoughts and Their Physical Effects on the Body

Our minds and bodies are not separate entities but rather partners in a constant dance of chemical messengers and electrical impulses. This interplay shapes our experiences of the world, for better or for worse. When our minds perceive a threat—like a car swerving into our lane or the news of a loved one's illness—our bodies respond with a surge of stress hormones, such as cortisol and adrenaline. This is the stress response, a survival mechanism designed to prepare us for fight or flight.

In the short term, this response is essential for survival, providing us with the energy and focus needed to navigate challenges. However, when stress becomes chronic, it can unleash a cascade of negative effects on our physical health. It's like a car stuck in high gear, revving its engine but going nowhere fast. The constant flood of stress hormones can lead to inflammation, disrupt sleep, weaken our immune system, and even contribute to chronic pain.

But it's not just major life events that trigger this response. Our thoughts, even seemingly harmless ones, can also activate it. Negative thought patterns, worries about the future, and ruminations about past hurts can keep us in a perpetual state of low-grade stress. This subtle but persistent activation can wear us down over time, manifesting as knots in our backs, headaches, unhealthy food choices to cope with spiraling emotions, fatigue, or even depression.

Understanding How Thoughts Influence Chronic Pain and Emotional States

For me, this mind-body connection became painfully clear through my relationship with my biological father, Adrian. While we lived nearby, even in the same apartment complex at one point, he was emotionally unavailable. This emotional neglect, though subtle, was deeply traumatic. As I grew older, the unresolved hurt and anger manifested as chronic tension and pain in my shoulders and neck, gallons of tears shed in private moments, and years of heartache. My body was screaming out the pain that my mind had tried to suppress for so long.

The emotional patterns I internalized from this early experience shaped my relationships with men, drawing me to partners who mirrored my father's emotional distance. I found myself repeatedly stranded in relationships devoid of the deep connection I craved, desperately trying to fill the void left by my father's absence. Each heartbreak, each instance of rejection and abandonment, only served to deepen the childhood wounds that had never fully healed.

This cycle of pain and longing continued for years, leaving me feeling trapped and hopeless. Finally, after enduring countless failed relationships, I reached a breaking point. I could no longer bear the weight of this unresolved hurt. Summoning all my courage, I decided to confront my father directly.

With a trembling hand, I dialed his number, my heart pounding in my chest. To my surprise, he answered. I had meticulously rehearsed my lines, preparing for a confrontation, but when I heard his voice, all the carefully crafted words vanished. All I could muster was a raw, vulnerable plea: "I think your absence is affecting my relationships with men, and I'm hurt by you."

There was a long pause on the other end of the line. Then, a simple response: "Okay, well, whatever I have to do to fix it." At that moment, something shifted within me. A flood of bottled-up emotions—anger, hurt, sadness—poured out of me. It was as if a dam had burst, releasing years of pent-up pain. But as the tears flowed, I also felt a sense of relief, a weight lifted from my shoulders.

This conversation marked the beginning of a new chapter in my relationship with my father, and more importantly, in my relationship with myself. By finally acknowledging and expressing my pain, I had taken a crucial step toward healing. It was a powerful reminder that addressing emotional pain isn't just essential for our mental well-being, but it's also inextricably linked to our physical health.

Rewiring Your Brain for a Pain-Free Life: The Power of the Reticular Activating System

The good news is that our brains aren't fixed entities; they possess an extraordinary capacity for change and adaptation, even in the face of chronic pain. This phenomenon, known as neuroplasticity, is like a hidden superpower within us, allowing us to rewire our neural pathways and create new patterns of thinking and feeling.

A key player in this process is the reticular activating system (RAS), a network of neurons in our brainstem that plays a crucial role in regulating arousal, attention, and sleep-wake cycles. While the RAS doesn't solely determine what we pay attention to, it does influence our focus by filtering sensory information and prioritizing stimuli that align with our current goals and needs.

Think of it like the rigorous training regimen my high school basketball coach put us through. Day after day, we ran the same drills over and over again. Some practices consisted of nothing but running for two hours straight. When we made it to the playoffs and were on our way to the state championship, he made us listen to the new Keyshia Cole album at every single practice. As high school students, we were sick of it. We couldn't understand why Coach Lewis would "torture" us like this when we were winning by 15-20 points by halftime in most games.

But one thing we did do was show up to every practice and follow his instructions with no hesitation. Little did we know, Coach Lewis was not just shaping our basketball skills; he was programming our RAS for greatness. The RAS is like a mental filter, determining what information our brains focus on and what we tune out. Through those grueling practices and countless repetitions, he was training our RAS to filter out distractions and hone in on the key elements of the game.

The lessons we learned from this experience were invaluable. Those running practices we hated paid off during the games because we had the endurance and stamina to outrun our opponents. And while we may have grumbled about listening to Keyshia Cole's album on repeat, it taught us to drown out the noise and focus on winning the game. The only voices we could hear on that court were Coach Lewis's and Ms. Natalie's, our assistant coach, guiding us toward victory. It was this unwavering focus, honed through repetition and discipline, that allowed us to filter out distractions and perform at our best.

In the same way, we can intentionally cultivate positive thought patterns through consistent practice, gradually rewiring our brains for greater resilience and well-being. By focusing our attention on the positive aspects of our lives and practicing gratitude, we can train our RAS to filter out negativity and amplify joy. It's like adjusting the dial on a radio, tuning in to a station that broadcasts a more uplifting message. And just as Coach Lewis transformed us into a state championship-worthy team, we can transform ourselves into champions of our own lives by harnessing the power of our RAS.

The Power of Your Subconscious Mind: Harnessing Your Inner Healer

Our subconscious mind, which I like to compare to the operating system running in the background of a computer, plays a pivotal role in shaping our thoughts and beliefs. It's like a hard drive, storing our deepest fears, desires, and memories, and influencing our behaviors and reactions in ways we may not even be aware of. What we store in this hard drive can significantly impact our lives, attracting experiences and situations that align with our subconscious programming.

Just as a skilled gardener carefully cultivates the soil to ensure a bountiful harvest, we must tend to our subconscious minds with intention and care. In his seminal work, *The Power of Your Subconscious Mind*, Joseph Murphy (2020) illuminates the transformative potential of this hidden realm within us. He teaches us that by harnessing the power of visualization, affirmations, and positive self-talk, we can align our conscious and subconscious minds, creating a harmonious symphony of thought and action.

With focused intention, we can reprogram our RAS, the brain's filter for information. By consciously choosing to focus on the positive aspects of our lives and replacing negative thoughts with empowering affirmations, we can effectively rewire our brains for greater resilience and well-being. It's like shedding an old, tattered garment and donning a new one, woven with threads of hope, self-belief, and unwavering optimism.

By identifying and overcoming subconscious blocks, we create space for our innate healing abilities to emerge. Like a phoenix rising from the ashes, we can transform our pain into power, our limitations into limitless potential. With each positive affirmation and each act of self-love, we water the seeds of change, allowing them to blossom into a life that's both fulfilling and extraordinary.

Awareness: The Catalyst for Change

Remember, your mind is a powerful tool. By understanding the connection between your thoughts and your physical well-being, you can take control of your health and create a life that's free from pain and full of joy.

Have you heard the saying, "When the student is ready, the teacher will appear"? (Tzu, n.d.). Well, I became a student to my teacher, Tim. I remember my first lesson vividly. I had taken a trip to NC A&T to watch my little brother, Morgan, graduate. Tim told me, "Just be the observer, just watch and don't talk much. The person in front of you always reflects to you who you are, the emotions you're holding inside of you." That weekend, I felt my family kept complaining, they were indecisive, and just angry. I had a brief break from my family and called Tim, saying, "There's no way this is a reflection of me." He replied, "This is you. What are you going to do to change it?"

I couldn't believe it, but I realized I couldn't change what I couldn't see or change my behavior if I didn't acknowledge that it was in me. Just as I had to confront my own negativity and complaining during my period of solitude, I had to recognize that the frustrations I saw in my family were a mirror reflecting aspects of myself that I needed to address. This awareness was the catalyst for change, the first step toward a more positive and fulfilling life.

In the following chapters, we'll delve deeper into specific techniques and practices that can help you harness the power of your mind to overcome pain, heal emotional wounds, and live a more fulfilling life. But for now, simply observe your thoughts. Notice how they make you feel, both physically and emotionally.

Chapter 2

Identifying Harmful Thought Patterns: The Power of Self-Reflection and the Path to Positive Change

What thoughts plague your mind that have you spiraling into a vortex of worry, your mind racing with worst-case scenarios? In my past relationships, these thoughts often echoed in my head: *This guy doesn't love me, otherwise he wouldn't treat me like this. If he loved me, he wouldn't leave me. If he loved me, he'd check on me.* It was a painful realization, but one of the first steps I learned in my healing journey was the power of "YOU."

We often want to blame the person on the outside, but that person is just reflecting back to us who we are. The universe will always give you what you're asking for, whether you see it as good or bad. I would always say, "He never calls me, he doesn't text me, he makes me feel like this." But the truth is, nobody can make you feel anything. You hold the power of your mind and emotions. My father Adrian was the catalyst for these thoughts, but I realized the change was up to me.

These experiences led me to recognize the insidious nature of negative thought patterns, those whispers of self-doubt that can erode our confidence and sabotage our happiness.

Recognizing the Shadows: Unveiling Negative Thought Patterns

Negative thoughts are like weeds in a garden. If left unchecked, they can quickly take over and choke out the beauty and vitality of our minds. These thoughts often take the form of self-criticism, worry, fear, or anger, triggered by stressful events, past traumas, or even seemingly insignificant daily situations.

For me, these negative thought patterns often revolved around my relationships, echoing the emotional neglect I felt from my father, Daddy Adrian. Despite his physical presence, his emotional absence left a void within me that I desperately tried to fill with love and validation from romantic partners. But this only led to a cycle of self-doubt and insecurity.

Thoughts like, *I know he's cheating, why do I keep accepting him back?* or *If he loved me, he wouldn't make me feel like this,* would plague my mind. I would rationalize his behavior, blaming myself for his shortcomings. *Maybe he doesn't think I'm pretty*, I'd think, despite the attention I received from other men. *Maybe he doesn't like the way I dress. I'll buy a better dress, and he will like it.*

These thoughts kept me stuck in a toxic cycle of self-blame and insecurity, chasing after love and acceptance that always seemed just out of reach. The pain of rejection and abandonment in these relationships mirrored the childhood wounds inflicted by my father's emotional distance. It was a painful realization, but one that ultimately led me on a path toward healing and self-discovery.

The first step in identifying negative thoughts is to become aware of them. This requires a willingness to observe our thoughts without judgment, simply noticing them as they arise. In the words of Napoleon Hill (2011), author of *Outwitting the Devil*, these negative thoughts can be likened to a cunning "devil" that seeks to sabotage our happiness and success by planting seeds of doubt and fear in our minds. While this may seem like a dramatic concept, it serves as a powerful reminder that negative thoughts can be insidious and destructive.

This period of intense introspection wasn't always easy. At first, my mind was a whirlwind of thoughts and emotions, a chaotic landscape of negativity and self-doubt. Questions like "Will I ever be okay with being by myself?" and "Do I even like myself if I can't be alone with myself?" haunted me relentlessly. It seemed the more I found myself and embraced self-love, the more distant people became.

But as the days turned into weeks and the weeks into months, a profound shift occurred. While the journey was slow and often painful, it was undoubtedly worth it. I began to see that the recurring thoughts of *Am I worthy of love?* or *Am I worthy of solace?* were not truths, but echoes of past hurts and insecurities, deeply ingrained in my subconscious.

From Shadows to Light: Transforming Destructive Thoughts

Once we've begun to recognize the shadows of negative thought patterns, it's essential to discern their nature and impact. Not all thoughts are created equal; some are productive, leading to positive action and growth, while others are destructive, causing harm and holding us back. The key is to learn to differentiate between the two.

Productive thoughts are often characterized by optimism, curiosity, and a sense of possibility. They inspire us to take action, try new things, and overcome challenges. They are the seeds of hope and resilience, fueling our personal growth and well-being.

Destructive thoughts, on the other hand, are often rooted in fear, self-doubt, and negativity. They can paralyze us, prevent us from taking risks, and keep us stuck in unhealthy patterns. They're the weeds that choke the life out of our dreams and aspirations. My feelings of unworthiness kept me in a state of feeling unloved and unsupported which prevented me from reaching my full potential. When we feel loved and supported, we feel as if all of our dreams can and will come true. There's no limit to what we can accomplish.

These destructive thought patterns can take many forms, each with its own unique way of distorting our reality and undermining our well-being. Some common patterns include:

☞ **All-or-Nothing Thinking:** This is when you see things in black and white terms, with no shades of gray. This type of thinking was evident in my relationships and friendships. If my friends and family didn't call me, I wouldn't call them. A friend constantly reinforced my negative thinking pattern that I wasn't loved if they didn't reach out. What you think, you attract, so the universe continued to have my phone not ring with phone calls and texts. This caused so much hurt and anger. The lesson learned was that I didn't need the constant calls and texts to feel validated or enough. When I got tired of being angry and hurt, I turned inward. Now that I completely love myself, my phone doesn't ring as much, but I am completely in love with myself. I give myself all my heart's desires, so if anyone else gives me anything, it's just extra.

☞ **Catastrophizing:** This is the tendency to exaggerate the negative consequences of events, blowing things out of proportion and focusing on the worst-case scenario. It's like a mental magnifying glass that amplifies our fears and anxieties, making them seem much larger than they actually are. I've always been nervous about public speaking, so when I signed up for Toastmasters and was asked to give my first speech the following week, my mind went into overdrive. I was consumed by thoughts like, *What if I forget everything I'm supposed to say? What if I freeze in front of the room? What if they all laugh at me?* Despite hours of preparation, I couldn't shake the feeling that I didn't know what I was doing. On the day of the speech, my nerves were shot. But as I finished speaking, I was met with applause and encouragement. People told me how well I'd done, and how engaging my speech was. It was a stark contrast to the catastrophic scenarios I had imagined. This experience taught me a valuable lesson: Our fears are often far worse than reality. By recognizing when we're catastrophizing, we can challenge those thoughts with a more balanced and realistic perspective, reducing unnecessary stress and anxiety.

☞ **Personalization**: This is when you blame yourself for things that aren't your fault. You might believe that you're responsible for other people's happiness or that their negative emotions are a direct result of your actions. In my own life, my father's emotional distance led me to a pattern of self-blame, as I internalized his behavior as a reflection of my own self-worth. His absence in my life led me to believe that I was unworthy of love and attention.

☞ **Mind Reading**: This is the tendency to assume we know what others are thinking or feeling without any concrete evidence. You might believe that someone is judging you negatively, even though they haven't said or done anything to show that. A tool I learned was to ask questions rather than jump to conclusions. Most people are preoccupied with their own thoughts and feelings, not yours. That judgment you feel is often just your own insecurities playing tricks on you. Stepping away from distractions and creating a morning routine of journaling, meditation, and listening to motivational content helped me reprogram my mind and focus on positivity.

We're not the clouds that pass through the sky of our consciousness; we're the vast sky itself, capable of holding both light and darkness. By cultivating this awareness, we can learn to navigate the ever-changing landscape of our minds with greater clarity, compassion, and wisdom. We can break free from the grip of destructive thought patterns and embrace a more positive and empowering mindset.

The Path to Liberation

The journey toward a more peaceful and empowered mind is not a destination, but an ongoing process of self-discovery and growth. It requires us to confront our shadows, challenge our assumptions, and embrace the vastness of our own consciousness. But as we learn to navigate the intricate landscape of our thoughts, we unlock a world of possibilities.

By stepping away from the distractions and demands of daily life, we create space for introspection and self-reflection. We begin to see our thoughts with greater clarity, recognizing the patterns that have held us captive for far too long. Stepping away from distractions helped me focus on myself and clear my mind of all the negative thought patterns. I began waking up at 4:45 am to journal, meditate, drink my cacao, meditate again, and while getting dressed, listen to motivational speeches on YouTube just to change my thought pattern. To reprogram my hard drive, I decided to dedicate 2 hours before work to focus on myself and listen to motivational speakers. I was rewired and ready to start my day positively.

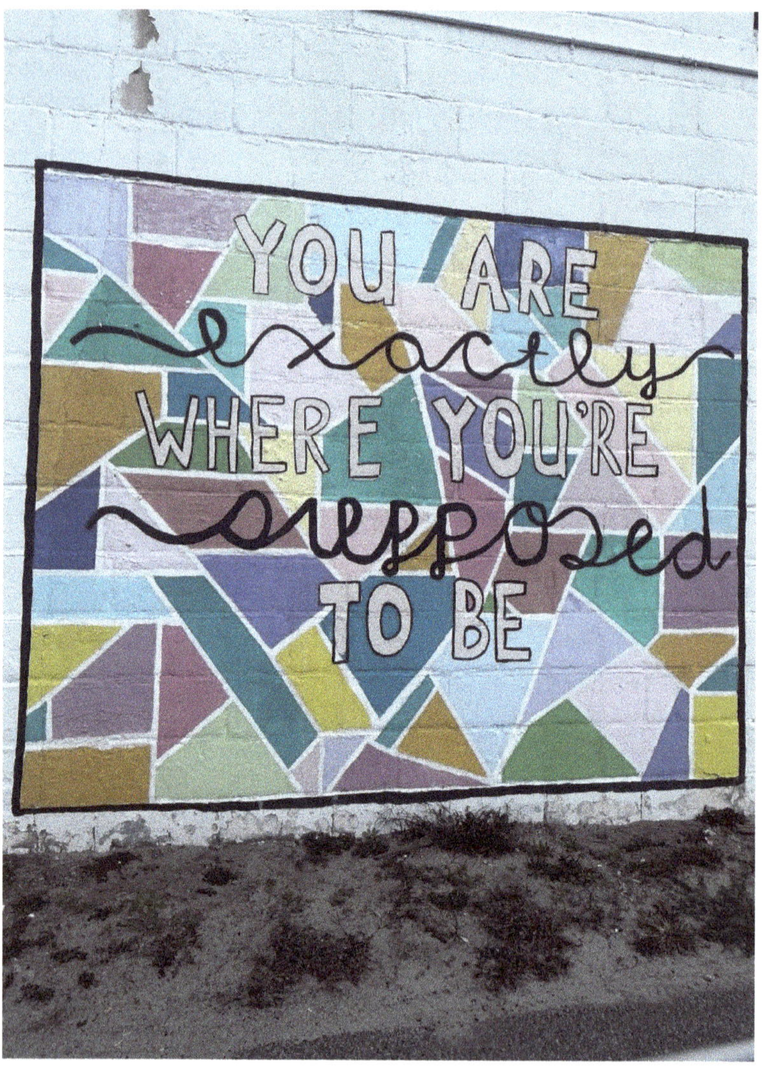

But solitude is just the beginning. To truly transform our minds, we must actively engage with our thoughts, challenging their validity and choosing to focus on those that empower and uplift us. This requires a willingness to step outside of our comfort zones, to experiment with new ways of thinking and being.

Sometimes the most unconventional methods can lead to the greatest breakthroughs. By embracing a beginner's mindset and approaching our thoughts with curiosity and openness, we can discover new perspectives and possibilities that were previously hidden from view. Jim Rohn (Prater, 2018), one of my favorite motivational speakers, always said:

> "Your personal philosophy is the greatest determining factor in how your life works out."

> "Don't wish it was easier, wish you were better. Don't wish for less problems, wish for more skills. Don't wish for less challenges, wish for more wisdom."

> "Success is nothing more than a few simple disciplines, practiced every day."

> "Motivation is what gets you started. Habit is what keeps you going."

> "Work harder on yourself than you do on your job."

These statements stuck with me. You can complain about the government and taxes, or you can learn the government's tax laws and use them in your favor. You can complain there are not enough hours in the day, or you can make better use of your time. When you change your philosophy, the entire world around you changes too. The universe will conspire in your favor to bring about change. It's up to you to accept or reject and be grateful however the experience shows up in your world.

The path ahead is illuminated by the promise of transformation. As we continue our journey, we'll explore a variety of tools and techniques that can help us rewire our brains for greater happiness and well-being. But before we move forward, let's take a moment to acknowledge the power of our own minds. Let's embrace both the shadows that lurk within and the light that shines through, for it's in this dance between darkness and light that we discover our true potential for healing, growth, and transformation.

Chapter 3

Principles of Cognitive Behavioral Therapy: Rewriting Your Inner Game

Imagine your mind as an athlete, constantly striving for peak performance. Just as athletes train their bodies to achieve physical prowess, we too can train our minds to unlock emotional resilience and well-being. In this chapter, we'll discover how cognitive behavioral therapy (CBT) acts as a personal trainer for your mind, equipping you with powerful tools and techniques to identify, challenge, and ultimately rewire unhelpful thought patterns.

CBT is a well-established, evidence-based form of psychotherapy that has shown remarkable success in treating a wide range of mental health conditions, from depression and anxiety to chronic pain. Its effectiveness lies in the fundamental principle that our thoughts, feelings, and behaviors are interconnected. By changing the way we think, we can profoundly transform how we feel and act.

Think of CBT as a mental gym where you'll engage in rigorous exercises designed to strengthen your cognitive muscles and build resilience. Just as a personal trainer pushes athletes beyond their comfort zones to achieve peak performance, CBT will challenge you to confront your negative thought patterns and replace them with healthier, more empowering beliefs.

Harnessing the Power of Thought: The CBT Approach

At the core of CBT is a process known as cognitive restructuring, a method for identifying and challenging unhelpful thoughts that can lead to negative emotions and behaviors. This process is like cleaning a dirty window: By removing the grime of negativity, we can see the world more clearly and respond to challenges with greater clarity and resilience.

But cognitive restructuring isn't the only tool in the CBT tool kit. Behavioral activation—the practice of engaging in activities that bring us pleasure and meaning, even when we don't feel motivated—plays a crucial role in rewiring our brains for happiness. This might seem counterintuitive, especially when we're feeling down. But just like Mr. Miyagi's seemingly unrelated training tasks in *The Karate Kid* secretly honed Daniel's karate skills, engaging in activities we enjoy can strengthen our mental muscles and rewire our brains for greater well-being.

CBT is a journey of self-discovery and transformation, one that requires trust, commitment, and a willingness to step outside of your comfort zone. But the rewards are immeasurable: greater emotional resilience, reduced stress, and a newfound sense of empowerment over your thoughts and feelings. So, just as Daniel-san learned to trust Mr.

Miyagi's unconventional methods, I invite you to trust the process of CBT. Let's explore its core principles and discover how you can apply them to create a life that's both joyful and resilient.

This mental training rests on three fundamental pillars:

1. **Awareness:** Just as a skilled athlete is keenly aware of their body's movements and adjusts their actions accordingly, CBT teaches us to cultivate a heightened awareness of our thoughts and emotions. This awareness allows us to identify negative thought patterns as they arise, creating an opportunity for intervention before they spiral out of control. For example, during my volleyball days, if I missed a few easy digs, I could feel frustration building within me. But I learned to catch this negative momentum early on, reminding myself with a simple mantra, "Just one pass. Just one pass." This helped me shift my focus back to the present moment, regain my composure, and get back in the game. Similarly, in life, noticing when you're caught in a spiral of negativity, without judgment or criticism, is the first step toward change. It's like shining a flashlight on the shadows of your mind, illuminating the patterns that need to be transformed.

2. **Challenge:** Once you've identified a negative thought, it's time to put it on trial. The father who raised me, Jerome, a strong Bahamian man, instilled in me the mantra, "Never let the boys see you cry." While this taught me resilience in the face

of adversity, it also inadvertently built a wall around my emotions, making it difficult to express vulnerability. I've learned to challenge this deeply ingrained belief, recognizing that true strength lies not in suppressing emotions but in embracing and expressing them authentically. Similarly, when a negative thought arises, put it on the stand and cross-examine it like a defense attorney. Ask yourself probing questions: "Is this thought based on facts or on unfounded fears? Is it serving me, or is it hindering my growth and well-being?" Questioning these thoughts, like a defense attorney cross-examining a witness, can help you uncover the distortions and biases that fuel negativity.

3. **Change:** The final step is to replace those unhelpful thoughts with more balanced and realistic ones. It's about rewriting your inner script and crafting a narrative that empowers you to face challenges with resilience and optimism. For me, this involved actively choosing to focus on my strengths and positive qualities. This shift in mindset allowed me to embrace my authentic self and experience a renewed sense of joy and purpose. Just as my intentional actions changed my internal landscape, you can also replace negative thoughts with positive ones, igniting a ripple effect that transforms your emotions and actions.

These three pillars form the foundation for a powerful tool kit of techniques that can help you reshape your mental landscape and cultivate greater well-being.

Tools for Transformation

Let's delve into the practical exercises that can help you put these principles into action and rewire your brain for a more positive and fulfilling life.

Thought Recording

Think of thought recording as a personal diary for your mind. It involves keeping a detailed log of your thoughts and feelings, noting the specific situations that trigger them, the emotions they evoke, and the behaviors that follow. This practice can help you identify patterns in your thinking and gain valuable insights into your emotional triggers.

During my period of isolation, my thought journal became a window into my deepest fears and insecurities. I found myself writing things like, "If they don't call me, I won't call them. I don't even care." These words revealed a pattern of defensiveness and emotional withdrawal, a protective armor I had built around my heart to shield myself from further pain. It reflected in a deep-seated fear of abandonment that had taken root in my mind.

But journaling also revealed something else: a glimmer of hope. As I poured my heart onto the pages, I began to recognize the power of words to shape my reality. I realized that my thoughts weren't immutable truths, but stories I was telling myself, stories that could be rewritten.

SIMPLY GRATEFUL
SIMPLY GRATEFUL

Inspired by this realization, I replaced my thought journal with a gratitude journal. Instead of focusing on my perceived shortcomings and the injustices of the world, I started writing about the things I was grateful for. It was a simple shift in focus, but it had a profound impact on my mindset.

Each morning, I would write down affirmations like: "I'm grateful for turning off the volume to my negative thoughts," "I'm open to receiving love and abundance," "I'm a doer, capable of achieving my goals," "I forgive myself and others, releasing the pain of the past," "My confidence is soaring," and "I acknowledge my own self-worth."

These affirmations were more than just words; they were seeds of positive transformation, planted in the fertile soil of my subconscious mind. As I repeated them day after day, they began to take root, gradually shifting my perspective and rewiring my brain for greater happiness and resilience.

Behavioral Experiments

While journaling and affirmations are powerful tools for internal transformation, sometimes we need to take our practice out into the real world. That's where behavioral experiments come in. These are actions we take to test the validity of our negative beliefs, to see if they hold up under scrutiny.

When a shaman suggested that I find hobbies and surround myself with loving people to overcome my anger and hurt over unanswered calls and texts, I was initially skeptical. But I decided to put her advice to the test. I started attending yoga classes and joined Toastmasters, a public speaking club.

To my surprise, these new activities not only brought me joy and a sense of community but also challenged my deeply held belief that I was "crazy" for expecting consistent communication from others. Through my interactions with the supportive and compassionate people I met, I realized that healthy relationships were indeed possible and that my past experiences didn't have to dictate my future.

These behavioral experiments, like the grueling basketball drills of my youth, pushed me outside of my comfort zone and forced me to confront my fears head-on. But just as those drills transformed me into a stronger and more skilled athlete, these exercises strengthened my mental muscles, equipping me with the tools to overcome challenges and create a more fulfilling life.

The Winning Mindset

In this chapter, we've learned that our thoughts, feelings, and behaviors are interconnected and that by challenging and changing our negative thought patterns, we can create lasting transformations in our lives. Just as athletes engage in rigorous training to enhance their physical performance, CBT offers a framework for mental training, honing our ability to manage stress, overcome challenges, and achieve our goals.

Throughout my athletic career, I never realized that the discipline and consistency I cultivated on the field would later become invaluable tools in my journey of personal growth. The practices on Sundays, waking up at 6 am, listening to Keyshia Cole during practice to ignore distractions, enduring two-a-days, or repeating the same rigorous drills over and over again—instilled in me a deep understanding of the power of perseverance and dedication.

When I decided to rewire my negative thought patterns, I tapped into that same athlete's mindset. I told myself, "If I can become a champion on the court, I can become a champion of my own mind." With that same discipline and consistency that had propelled me to athletic success, I embarked on a journey of mental transformation. I replaced self-doubt with self-belief, fear with courage, and negativity with gratitude. And just like those countless hours of practice had transformed me into a skilled athlete, this consistent effort to rewire my mind led to a profound shift in my overall well-being.

As you embark on your own journey of thought modification, remember that you're not alone. Whether you seek guidance from a therapist or choose to explore self-directed techniques, the most important thing is to find an approach that resonates with you. And just like any athlete, remember that the key to success lies in discipline, consistency, and the unwavering belief that you have the power to transform your mind and create a life that's both joyful and fulfilling.

Chapter 4

Awakening Presence:
A Mindful Journey to Wholeness

Have you ever found yourself scrolling through your phone, mindlessly consuming information, yet feeling utterly disconnected from the present moment? Or perhaps you've stood in line at the grocery store, heart pounding with anxiety about deadlines and to-do lists, while your surroundings fade into a blur. In our hyper-connected, fast-paced world, these experiences are all too common. We've become masters of multitasking, yet paradoxically, we often struggle to truly be present in our own lives.

I know I have. There have been countless times when I've been so consumed by the noise of my own thoughts that I've missed the beauty of a sunset, the warmth of a hug, or the simple joy of a shared meal. It's as if our modern advancements—while offering incredible convenience and connection—have also robbed us of something precious: the ability to simply be.

But what if there were a way to reclaim that presence? A practice that could anchor us in the present moment, calm the relentless chatter of our minds, and reconnect us with our inner wisdom? This is where mindfulness comes in. Rooted in ancient contemplative traditions, mindfulness has been practiced for centuries as a path toward greater awareness, compassion, and inner peace. Now it's emerging as a powerful antidote to the stress and disconnection of our modern lives.

Mindfulness: A Path to Wholeness

Mindfulness isn't just a trendy buzzword; it's a profound shift in how we relate to our experiences. It's about noticing your thoughts, feelings, bodily sensations, and the world around you without getting tangled up in judgments or worries. Picture your thoughts as clouds drifting across the sky—sometimes fluffy and light, other times dark and heavy, but always just passing through.

Have you ever pondered the origin of those thoughts? We have around 60,000-70,000 thoughts a day, but how many are truly ours? Our thoughts are shaped by the words we hear and the environment we're in. Let me tell you about my friend Debbie, who lives in New York. She has 30 cousins who are Puerto Rican, and none of them speak Spanish. However, all of them have a Spanish accent. Why? Because they learned to speak from their Spanish-speaking parents and grandparents. It's a perfect example of how our surroundings can influence our thoughts and behaviors.

But mindfulness isn't about achieving a blank mind or reaching some state of blissful detachment. It's about accepting whatever comes up in your mind, whether it's good or bad, without trying to change it or push it away. This acceptance creates space around our experiences, giving us the freedom to choose how we respond instead of reacting impulsively.

Nourishing Body and Mind: A Holistic Approach

As we embark on this mindful journey, it's essential to recognize that true well-being encompasses not just our minds, but also our bodies and spirits. It means nourishing ourselves with wholesome foods, engaging in joyful movement, and cultivating a lifestyle that supports our overall health and happiness.

Deepak Chopra's *The Seven Spiritual Laws of Success* (2008) was a guiding light, opening my eyes to the interconnectedness of all aspects of our being and the importance of aligning our actions with our deepest values and aspirations. The book emphasizes the principle of giving and receiving. Just as we nourish our bodies with healthy food, we must also nourish our minds and spirits with positive thoughts, loving relationships, and meaningful experiences. And just as we receive the benefits of exercise in the form of increased energy and vitality, we must also give back to ourselves and others through acts of kindness, compassion, and service.

The Power of Food: Mindful Eating

Food isn't just fuel; it's a source of nourishment, pleasure, and connection. Yet, how often do we eat our meals on autopilot, barely tasting the flavors or noticing the textures? Mindful eating invites us to slow down and savor each bite, engaging all of our senses.

I vividly remember my mindful meals in my high-rise apartment. I would set the scene, plating my food beautifully using my gold utensils, the warm glow of the sunset filtering through my floor-to-ceiling windows. Chris-n-Teeb's *Perfect* would play in the background, its opening lyrics a reminder that "I'm blessed, I genuinely love my company." These moments were a celebration of self-care, a reminder that I was worthy of nourishment and enjoyment.

Mindful eating is not about denying yourself pleasure or limiting your food choices; it's about cultivating a deeper awareness of our relationship with food. By slowing down and paying attention, we can discover new flavors, textures, and aromas that we might have missed before. We can also learn to tune in to our body's hunger and fullness cues, eating only when we're truly hungry and stopping when we're satisfied. This practice not only enhances our enjoyment of food but also helps us make healthier choices and develop a more positive relationship with our bodies.

Mindful eating also involves paying attention to the nutritional value of our food. By choosing whole, unprocessed foods that nourish our bodies, we can improve our physical and mental health, reduce inflammation, and boost our energy levels.

น้ำส้ม
ORANGE JUICE

Moving Toward Joy: Mindful Movement

Just as mindful eating can transform our relationship with food, mindful movement can transform our relationship with our bodies. Exercise isn't just about building muscle and burning calories; it's about releasing endorphins, our body's natural painkillers and mood boosters. It's about feeling strong, confident, and capable in our own bodies.

Walking has become my moving meditation, a sanctuary for both body and mind. Whether I'm wrestling with writer's block, plotting my next adventure, or facing a difficult decision, I find solace and clarity in the rhythmic cadence of my steps. Each footfall anchors me to the present moment, connecting me to the earth below and the sky above.

The sights, sounds, and sensations of nature envelop me as I walk. The vibrant tapestry of trees and flowers unfurls before my eyes; each blossom a testament to the beauty of life. The symphony of birdsong, the gentle rustle of leaves, and even the distant hum of traffic, all weave together to create a soundtrack for my journey. I breathe in the crisp air, feel the sun's warmth on my skin, and relish the grounding sensation of grass beneath my feet.

If my thoughts drift, I turn to audiobooks or sermons, transforming my walk into a mobile classroom. I set goals for myself—perhaps to complete a chapter or a specific distance—using these milestones to maintain focus and motivation. In this way, walking becomes not just an exercise for my body, but also nourishment for my mind and spirit.

Beyond walking, mindful movement can take many forms. It could be dancing to your favorite music, practicing yoga, or simply stretching and breathing deeply. The key is to find activities that you enjoy and that allow you to be fully present in your body. As you move, pay attention to the sensations in your muscles and joints, the rhythm of your breath, and the way your body feels in space. Notice any tension or discomfort and gently release it.

The Power of Intention: Manifestation Through Mindfulness

Mindfulness has been a transformative force in my life, not only in managing emotional pain but also in opening me up to the remarkable power of intention and manifestation. It's as if by cultivating present-moment awareness, I've also awakened a deeper connection to the universe and its subtle workings.

This newfound awareness has led to numerous experiences where my intentions seemed to manifest into reality. Once, after resisting the temptation of Tiff's Treats cookies, I was surprised to find three boxes waiting for me at a client's house later that evening. Another time, my heartfelt desire to become a traveling nanny for a family I adored materialized into an invitation to join them on a trip to Turks and Caicos. Even a simple wish for a four-day weekend for my birthday came true effortlessly.

These experiences have taught me that our thoughts and feelings have the power to shape our reality. As the saying goes, "What you think, you become. What you feel, you attract. What you imagine, you create" (Buddha, n.d.).

Mindfulness allows us to tap into this power by becoming more aware of our thoughts and feelings, and consciously choosing those that align with our deepest desires. It's about recognizing that we're co-creators of our lives and that through intention and focused attention, we can manifest our dreams into reality.

Creating a Lifestyle of Health and Happiness

The power of intention is a cornerstone of mindfulness, weaving its magic not only in manifesting our dreams but also in cultivating a healthier, happier lifestyle. It's about aligning our actions with our deepest values and desires and making conscious choices that nourish our bodies, minds, and spirits.

Creating lasting change isn't about overnight transformations; it's about embracing a journey of small, intentional steps. I remember when I first set out to make healthier choices, it felt overwhelming. However, I soon realized that lasting change comes from building new habits gradually. If you intend to incorporate more exercise, start with two or three workouts a week and slowly increase the frequency. Craving healthier food? Begin by planning your meals and stocking your pantry with nutritious options. These small victories build momentum and make the journey sustainable.

Integrating mindfulness into your daily routine is another key ingredient in this recipe for well-being. Life is busy, and distractions are everywhere, but by setting reminders or alarms on your phone, you can create intentional pauses throughout the day to check in with yourself. These moments of mindfulness can be as simple as taking a few deep breaths, repeating a positive affirmation, or simply noticing the sensations in your body.

One helpful tip is to set reminders or alarms to prompt you to pause and practice mindfulness throughout the day. I would set reminders in my phone to go off each hour throughout the day starting from the time I got to work at 7:00 am, each reminding me with affirmations like:

- ☞ "I'm a doer. I'll take action and get things accomplished."

- ☞ "I acknowledge my own self-worth and my confidence is soaring."

- ☞ "I deserve love, compassion, and empathy."

- ☞ "I matter. I'm allowed to say no to others and yes to myself."

- ☞ "I honor my commitment to myself."

- ☞ "My body doesn't define me. Be kind to yourself. You have been through a lot."

These affirmations served as anchors, reminding me of my inherent worth and capacity for growth. They helped me cultivate self-compassion, especially on days when I struggled to stay on track.

Remember, mindfulness is a practice, not a destination. There will be setbacks and challenges along the way. But with persistence, self-compassion, and a willingness to start small, you can weave mindfulness into the fabric of your life, creating a foundation for lasting health and happiness.

Embracing the Now

Mindfulness is a lifelong journey of self-discovery and growth, a path toward greater awareness, compassion, and inner peace. By integrating mindfulness into our daily lives, we can transform even the most mundane activities into opportunities for presence, joy, and connection. Whether it's savoring a meal or taking a mindful walk, each moment becomes a chance to cultivate a deeper connection with ourselves and the world.

As you embark on this journey, remember that mindfulness is a practice, not a destination. It's about showing up for yourself, moment by moment, with curiosity, kindness, and an open heart. Through consistent practice, you'll discover the transformative power of mindfulness to reduce pain, manage stress, and cultivate a more joyful and fulfilling life.

In the next chapter, we'll turn our attention to building emotional resilience and exploring techniques and practices that can help you navigate life's challenges with greater strength and grace.

Chapter 5

Building Emotional Resilience

Remember that emotional roller coaster of a relationship, the one where the person felt so close yet so far away? For me, this wasn't a one-time experience; it was a recurring pattern. The faces changed, but the feelings remained the same. The universe kept serving up similar experiences, and after my fifth relationship, it hit me: I was the common denominator. I was the one attracting these situations.

These relationships were a whirlwind of exhilarating highs and devastating lows. One day, I'd be dreaming of a future filled with love, marriage, and children. The next, he'd vanish for days, leaving me shattered, abandoned, and questioning my worth. This was an echo of the pain I felt growing up with my dad Adrian's emotional absence.

The final months of each relationship were agonizing. I'd sob myself to sleep, clutching my chest, wondering why I kept attracting men who mirrored my father's emotional distance. But every time, I'd let him back in, hoping for a different outcome. It took a year to finally say "enough is enough" in each of those relationships.

You might be thinking, *A year? And five relationships later?* But life is a journey of experiences, and growth takes time. We're constantly evolving. When you're truly ready to change, you'll recognize the signs sooner. For me, it went from a year to six months, then six weeks, then three days, then one. Now, I can often tell within the initial conversations whether we align. If I can't have an open and honest conversation, there's no way I'm going on a date.

Through these heartbreaks, I discovered that resilience is the inner strength that allows us to bounce back from setbacks, learn from our mistakes, and keep moving forward, even when the path ahead is uncertain. You become unstoppable when you embrace the unknown, trusting your ability to navigate life's challenges.

In this chapter, we'll delve into the art of building emotional resilience. We'll explore tools and techniques, from simple breathing exercises to powerful mindfulness practices, that can help you cultivate this inner strength.

Nurturing Your Inner Strength: Simple Tools for Emotional Resilience

Emotional resilience isn't about being stoic or suppressing our feelings; it's about learning to navigate the inevitable storms of life with grace and strength. It's about cultivating an inner reservoir of calm and courage that we can draw upon when faced with challenges, setbacks, or pain. Think of it like a muscle—the more we use it, the stronger it becomes. Just like physical exercise builds our bodies, certain practices can fortify our emotional resilience, allowing us to bounce back from adversity and thrive in the face of life's uncertainties.

Let's explore some simple yet powerful techniques that can help you nurture your inner strength and build emotional resilience.

Deep Breathing: Your Anchor in the Storm

In moments of stress or overwhelm, our breath often becomes shallow and rapid, fueling the fight-or-flight response. But by consciously slowing down and deepening our breath, we can activate the parasympathetic nervous system, our body's natural calming mechanism.

After reflecting on my family's behavior at my little brother's graduation, I began to observe my experiences more closely. When someone responded aggressively, I checked my own inner energy and realized my cells were jumping. I was angry, and the person in front of me was simply mirroring that energy back. This wasn't easy to grasp, and it took practice and consistency to change.

Think about those frustrating calls to customer service, where your needs aren't being met and you're not getting your way. Remember that feeling of rising anger and frustration, much like a child denied their desires? These calls became my training ground. When I started responding with kindness, calmness, and love, while clearly stating my needs, I got different results. Life felt easier. I learned to pause before reacting, and to not get caught up in the perceived "drama" of the situation. As I shifted my energy, I started attracting the things I truly wanted and desired.

Now, when frustration arises, I recognize it immediately. I shift my energy and respond with kindness, calmness, and love. Try it—it can transform your entire experience.

Picture yourself next to a peaceful lake, feeling a gentle breeze on your skin as you take a deep breath. Feel your abdomen expand as you fill your lungs with air, and then slowly release it, letting go of tension and worry with each exhale. Repeat this several times, allowing your breath to anchor you in the present moment and restore a sense of peace and calm.

The Rhythm of Resilience: Finding Solace in Dance

Growing up in a Bahamian household filled with the vibrant sounds of soca and reggae, dance was woven into the fabric of my life. The dad who raised me, Daddy Jerome, would teach me his favorite moves, and we'd whine our hips and go low to the infectious rhythms that filled our home. It was pure joy, a celebration of life, love, and happiness.

In my darkest moments, when I felt lost and disconnected, I turned back to this childhood passion. Dance became my therapy, a way to release pent-up emotions, reduce stress and anxiety, and uplift my spirits. The rhythmic movements allowed me to express myself authentically, to reconnect with my body and my inner joy.

But dance did more than just lift my mood; it helped me rewire my brain. I realized that the music I listened to had a profound impact on my emotional state. The lyrics of popular songs, often filled with negativity and self-destructive messages, were fueling my own negative thought patterns.

After attending a retreat, I discovered a new genre of music—one that was softer, more loving, and filled with positive affirmations. It was like a balm for my soul, gently washing away the negativity and replacing it with a sense of hope and empowerment. I started listening to artists like Tyla Jane, Toni Jones, Londrelle, and Peachkka, whose lyrics spoke of self-love, resilience, and spiritual protection.

I even incorporated these empowering lyrics into my dance practice, singing them aloud as I moved my body. It was like a mantra, a way to reprogram my subconscious mind and cultivate a more positive outlook on life. And as I danced to these uplifting rhythms, I felt a shift within myself. I became more confident, more self-assured, and more resilient in the face of challenges.

Guided Imagery: Manifesting Your Dreams

Our minds are capable of conjuring vivid images and sensations that can transport us to another world. Guided imagery harnesses this power, inviting us to visualize peaceful and calming scenes that can soothe our souls and ease our pain. But it can also be used to manifest our desires and create a new reality for ourselves.

Not all my relationships were bad. There was this guy, Josh, who I had known since elementary school. He could see me for me. He saw me from the inside out. Most people just see my beauty and sexualize me. He never did this; he loved me from day one. One thing I liked about him the most was how he would imagine with me. He would always talk about us getting married, having kids, being so loving to our kids, and all the smart technology we would have in our house. He taught me how to see things to manifest them.

In my time in isolation, I added imagery to my daily routine. I remember lying in bed during my meditation and envisioning the next place I would live. I saw myself in a home with a blue kitchen with gold fixtures and black and white tiles, as this is a sign of the wealthy. A few days later, I went to a client's house to cover a date night for a new family that I now work for. I walked into this lovely home in Buckhead, and the first sign of my manifestation was the black and white tiles as soon as I walked through the front door. Oh, and it didn't stop there! She walked me to the kitchen, and there it was, the blue kitchen with the gold fixtures. I thought, *Wow, all my practice imagining manifested through this family.*

Close your eyes and imagine yourself strolling along a pristine beach, the warm sand between your toes and the sound of waves gently lapping at the shore. Breathe in the salty air, feel the sun on your skin, and let your worries drift away with the tide. Or perhaps you envision yourself nestled in a cozy cabin in the woods, a crackling fire warming your face as you sip a cup of herbal tea. Whatever scene resonates with you, allow yourself to fully immerse in it, savoring the peace and tranquility it brings.

Resilience Rises: A Journey Guided by Wisdom

The primary cause of unhappiness is never the situation but your thoughts about it. Be aware of the thoughts you are thinking. Separate them from the situation, which is always neutral. It is as it is.

–Eckhart Tolle

The tools we've explored, like deep breathing and guided imagery, are like trusty companions on our journey toward emotional resilience. They provide immediate relief and help us build a foundation of inner strength. But true resilience goes beyond managing our reactions to stressors; it's about cultivating a mindset and lifestyle that allows us to thrive in the face of adversity.

A book that deeply impacted my journey is Don Miguel Ruiz's *The Four Agreements*. In it, he outlines four simple yet powerful principles for personal transformation:

1. **Be Impeccable With Your Words:** Speak with integrity and avoid using words to harm yourself or others. Our words hold immense power, capable of

uplifting or tearing down. I began journaling affirmations like, "I love how I light up rooms when I walk in," "I love how I shine so bright," and "I show myself the love I deserve." When feelings of loneliness crept in, I countered them with, "There's so much love around me," repeating it six times to negate the negative thought. By choosing our words carefully and speaking with kindness and compassion, we not only create a more positive environment for ourselves and others, but we also strengthen our own sense of self-worth and integrity.

2. **Don't Take Anything Personally:** What others say and do is a projection of their own reality, not yours. When we take things personally, we give away our power and allow the opinions and actions of others to dictate our emotional state. I learned this lesson through a relationship with a man named Devin. He always prioritized his own needs, which I initially took personally as a sign that he didn't care about me. However, after the relationship ended, I realized his actions were a reflection of his own journey, not a judgment of my worth.

3. **Don't Make Assumptions:** Communicate clearly to avoid misunderstandings. Misunderstandings are often at the root of conflict and hurt feelings. By communicating openly and honestly, and seeking clarification when needed, we can build stronger relationships and avoid unnecessary

drama. I experienced this firsthand with new friends at Toastmasters. When they held a book club meeting without me, I felt hurt and excluded. But after communicating my feelings, I learned it was an oversight, not a deliberate exclusion. We could resolve the misunderstanding and strengthen our friendship.

4. **Always Do Your Best:** Your best will vary from moment to moment, but always strive to do your best. Striving for excellence in everything we do, whether it's a work project or a simple act of kindness, fosters a sense of pride and accomplishment. And even when we fall short, we can take comfort in knowing that we gave it our all.

By applying these principles to our lives, we cultivate greater emotional resilience. We become less reactive to external events, more grounded in our own truth, and more confident in our ability to navigate life's challenges.

The Power of the Pen: Journaling Your Way to Resilience

One powerful tool for integrating these principles and fostering resilience is journaling. It's more than just writing down thoughts; it's a means of self-discovery, emotional processing, and personal growth. While practices like deep breathing offer immediate relief, journaling helps us delve deeper, understanding the root causes of our emotions and reactions.

Think of your journal as a haven, a private sanctuary where you can be completely honest with yourself without fear of judgment. It's a space to explore your fears, celebrate your triumphs, and process difficult emotions. By putting your thoughts and feelings into words, you gain clarity, perspective, and a sense of control over your inner world.

Here are a few journaling prompts to spark your journey:

- ☞ **Emotional Check-In:** What am I feeling right now? What triggered these emotions? How can I respond to them in a healthy way?

- ☞ **Gratitude Practice:** What am I grateful for today? What small joys or blessings can I appreciate?

- ☞ **Future Visioning:** What are my dreams and aspirations? What steps can I take today to move closer to those goals?

- ☞ **Challenge Reflection:** What challenges have I faced recently? What did I learn from them? How did I grow as a result?

Remember, there are no right or wrong answers when it comes to journaling. It's simply a process of exploration and self-expression. The key is to be honest, open, and non-judgmental toward yourself. Allow your thoughts and feelings to flow freely onto the page, without trying to censor or edit them.

By making journaling a daily habit, you create a powerful tool for building resilience. You develop a deeper understanding of yourself, your triggers, and your patterns of behavior. This awareness empowers you to make conscious choices that align with your values and goals, even in the face of adversity.

So, grab a pen and paper—or open up a digital journaling app—and start writing your way to resilience. It's a journey of self-discovery that can transform your life.

Chapter 6

Navigating Setbacks and Cultivating Joy: The Resilient Path to Happiness

You've climbed mountains, conquered inner demons, and basked in the sunlight of personal triumphs. Yet, even in moments of seeming victory, an undertow tugs at your ankles, threatening to drag you back into the depths of old patterns and pain. Relapse, that unwelcome specter, can haunt even the most dedicated traveler on the path of self-improvement.

But what if relapse wasn't the enemy, but a teacher disguised in shadow? What if those painful detours held the key to unlocking even greater resilience and wisdom? As I often remind myself, "Love always gets better, and life always gets better. If you can see it, if you believe it, you can manifest it." Perhaps these setbacks are not roadblocks, but opportunities for growth, and chances to deepen our understanding of ourselves and our journey. In this chapter, we embark on a journey of radical acceptance, acknowledging the reality of setbacks as part of the human experience. We'll learn to decode the triggers that can send us spiraling, create a personalized tool kit for navigating turbulent emotional waters, and transform the energy of relapse into fuel for our ongoing transformation. We'll even delve into the spiritual teachings that illuminate the hidden purpose behind our struggles, revealing a path toward deeper healing and unwavering strength.

Embracing the Undertow: A Compass for Navigating Relapse

The first step in overcoming relapse is understanding its nature. It's not a sign of weakness or failure, but a natural ebb and flow in the tides of our emotional lives. By acknowledging this reality, we can approach setbacks with curiosity rather than judgment, transforming them into opportunities for growth.

The Anatomy of a Relapse: Unveiling Your Personal Triggers

Let's face it: We all have those moments when the ghosts of our past come knocking. Maybe it's a familiar pang of self-doubt after a minor setback, a surge of anger triggered by a seemingly harmless comment, or a full-blown emotional meltdown when life throws us a curveball. These are our "relapse triggers," the subtle (or not-so-subtle) cues that can send us spiraling back into old patterns of thinking and behavior.

The first step to navigating these treacherous waters is to become an emotional detective, uncovering the unique triggers that lie beneath the surface of our own psyches. For me, it was the gnawing ache of loneliness and isolation that threatened to unravel my hard-won progress. I found myself craving the numbing comfort of old habits, the familiar scripts of self-deprecation that had once been my constant companions.

To break free from the cycle of relapse, I embarked on a journey of self-discovery, one that involved confronting my deepest fears and insecurities. This meant peeling back the layers of my emotional landscape, meticulously documenting the situations, thoughts, and emotions that seemed to precede my relapses. It was a raw and sometimes painful process, requiring a level of brutal honesty that I wasn't always comfortable with. But as I delved deeper into my own psyche, I began to see patterns emerge.

I realized that my most potent triggers were often rooted in my fear of being alone. A canceled dinner date, a quiet evening at home, even a moment of introspection—these could all spark a wave of anxiety and self-doubt, threatening to pull me back into old, destructive patterns. Armed with this newfound awareness, I could start crafting a relapse prevention plan that addressed the root of the problem, rather than simply trying to mask the symptoms.

One strategy that proved incredibly powerful was to actively challenge my fear of solitude. I started scheduling weekly solo dates with myself, indulging in two of my favorite things: eating and relaxing. These outings weren't just about pampering myself; they were about reclaiming my independence and proving to myself that I could enjoy life on my own terms.

I even pushed myself to face one of my biggest fears: dining alone. In the past, I would always call a friend to keep me company, using the conversation as a crutch to avoid facing my own discomfort. But on this journey of self-discovery, I vowed to break free from this habit. I remember a particularly challenging moment during a trip to France with a client. I had a free day to explore on my own, but the fear of being alone in a foreign country was almost paralyzing. I found myself reaching for my phone to call my mentor, Tim, for support.

As we talked, I realized that this fear was more than just a dislike of solo dining; it was a reflection of a deeper insecurity, a belief that I wasn't enough on my own. I promised myself: "This is just the beginning. One day, you won't need a phone call to be comfortable when you go out on your own. One day, you won't need a FaceTime call to enjoy a dinner that's supposed to be spent alone."

Inspired by his encouragement, I took a deep breath and stepped out into the unknown. I wandered through charming cobblestone streets and savored delicious pastries at a local cafe. By the end of the day, I felt a newfound sense of confidence and independence. It was a small victory, but it marked a turning point in my journey toward self-acceptance and resilience.

As I continued to face my fears head-on, the frequency and intensity of my relapses diminished. I learned to embrace solitude as a gift, a sacred space where I could connect with my innermost self, nurture my creativity, and cultivate a deeper sense of self-love. And as I grew more comfortable in my own skin, I found I was less likely to be triggered by external events or the opinions of others.

Silencing the Inner Critic: Rewriting the Script of Your Mind

Even with the best-laid plans, that pesky inner critic can still manage to crash the party. You know, that voice that whispers, "You're not good enough," or "You'll never succeed." It's like having an uninvited guest who just won't leave. But here's the thing: You don't have to let that voice dictate the narrative of your life.

Think of it like this: You're the director of your own mental movie. And if the scene starts to get too dark and twisty, you have the power to yell "Cut!" That's where the technique of thought-stopping comes in. It's your mental emergency brake, a way to slam on the brakes when those negative thoughts start to gain momentum.

The moment you catch that inner critic whispering, interrupt the pattern with a firm and resounding "Stop!" Say it out loud, whisper it under your breath, or even just think it with every ounce of conviction you can muster. Then comes the fun part: Replace that negative thought with a positive affirmation, your own personal power mantra.

For me, when I start to spiral into self-doubt, I like to repeat the affirmation "I am capable and resilient, and I can overcome any challenge" at least seven times. It might sound silly at first, but trust me, the repetition works wonders. It's like replacing the old, worn-out tapes of negativity with a fresh, empowering soundtrack.

Another trick I've found incredibly helpful is reframing my perspective. It's all about looking at the situation through a different lens like a photographer adjusting their focus to capture a new angle. Instead of seeing a setback as a sign of personal failure, I try to view it as a hidden opportunity, a chance to learn and grow.

Remember, we've already established that our thoughts have a profound impact on our reality. So why not choose thoughts that uplift and empower us? By consciously choosing to focus on the positive and reframe our challenges, we can transform our inner dialogue from a source of self-sabotage into a wellspring of resilience and unwavering self-belief.

The Sacred Art of Forgiveness: Unburdening the Heart

Thought-stopping and reframing are like trusty tools in my emotional toolbox, but I've learned that true resilience often requires something more profound—a journey into the spiritual depths of our being. For me, this path led me to the transformative wisdom of Neale Donald Walsch's *Conversations With God* (1995).

In this extraordinary book, Walsch delves into the very nature of suffering and the incredible power of forgiveness. He paints a picture of life's experiences, both joyful and painful, as purposeful lessons meticulously designed to guide our evolution. When obstacles arise, we're faced with a crucial choice: to surrender to the depths of despair or to rise above the challenge, emerging stronger and more enlightened.

Walsch's teachings resonated with me on a soul-deep level, particularly his emphasis on forgiveness. I came to understand that true forgiveness isn't about excusing harmful behavior or erasing the past; it's about liberating ourselves from the emotional baggage that weighs us down. It's about acknowledging our pain, honoring our feelings, and then consciously choosing to release the anger, resentment, and blame that keep us shackled to old wounds.

For me, this meant embarking on a long and arduous journey of forgiving myself and everybody that hurt me. It wasn't easy, and there were countless tears shed along the way. But by facing my pain head-on and choosing to let go of the anger I had carried for so many years, I was finally able to cultivate a more compassionate and understanding relationship with both myself and my father.

This experience taught me that forgiveness isn't something we do for others; it's something we do for ourselves. It's an act of self-preservation, a way to break free from the chains of the past and reclaim our power. When we forgive, we liberate ourselves from the role of victim and step into the role of creator, empowered to shape our own destinies.

This wisdom can serve as a guiding light on your own journey of resilience. When you encounter setbacks, remember that they're not roadblocks, but stepping stones. Embrace them with an open heart, eager to learn the lessons they hold. Forgive yourself for past mistakes, recognizing that you're a work in progress, always evolving and growing. Above all, cultivate a deeper connection to your spiritual self, drawing strength and guidance from whatever source resonates with you.

Whether it's God, the universe, or simply the interconnectedness of all living beings, this connection can provide you with a sense of peace, purpose, and belonging that transcends the challenges of everyday life. It's a reminder that even in our darkest moments, we're never truly alone, and that there's always a flicker of light guiding us toward healing and wholeness.

The Alchemy of Happiness: Turning Setbacks Into Stepping Stones

Having weathered the storms of setbacks and emerged stronger on the other side, it's time to shift our focus to the sunnier shores of happiness. This isn't about chasing fleeting pleasures or pretending that pain doesn't exist. It's about cultivating a deep-rooted joy that can withstand life's inevitable storms.

Michael A. Singer's *The Untethered Soul* (2007) became my compass on this leg of the journey. It taught me that happiness isn't something we find "out there" but a state of being we nurture within. Singer's words encouraged me to release the grip of inner turmoil that had kept me trapped in a cycle of suffering and to embrace a life of genuine contentment.

His teachings emphasized the importance of mindfulness and detachment—of observing our thoughts and emotions without judgment. By creating space between ourselves and our inner experiences, we gain the freedom to choose how we respond to them. This detachment, I discovered, is like a key that unlocks the door to inner peace and joy.

But the real magic lies in learning to keep our hearts open, even when faced with adversity. It's easy to shut down, to build walls around our hearts when we've been hurt. But in doing so, we also block out the very things that make life worth living—love, joy, and connection. To truly experience the full spectrum of human emotions, we must embrace both the light and the dark, allowing all of our feelings to flow through us like a river, rather than damming them up and creating internal chaos.

Singer's (n.d.) words resonated with me: "Notice that you aren't asking how to get rid of the problem; you're asking how to protect yourself from feeling it." It was a powerful reminder that true healing comes not from avoiding pain, but from embracing it, allowing it to move through us and ultimately transform us.

Practical Steps to Cultivate Happiness

Mindfulness and self-awareness are the foundation of a joyful life, but they're just the beginning. There are countless other practices and strategies we can weave into our daily routines to nurture happiness and contentment.

1. **Embrace Gratitude:** Gratitude is a powerful antidote to negativity. By focusing on the good in our lives, we shift our perspective from scarcity to abundance. This doesn't mean ignoring our challenges but choosing to focus on the blessings that surround us. The simple act of writing an entire page in my gratitude journal about what I was grateful for each day transformed my outlook on life. You can start with five things you're grateful for each day, and as you practice gratitude, you'll find it easier to see the beauty and abundance that's always present.

2. **Nurture Positive Relationships:** Our relationships with others play a crucial role in our emotional well-being. Surround yourself with people who uplift and inspire you, who believe in your dreams and support your journey. During my college years, I was fortunate to be part of both the volleyball and softball teams, where I experienced the power of collaboration and teamwork firsthand. The girls on the team looked to me for advice on everything from improving their game to securing a starting position. Together, we worked tirelessly toward our shared goal of winning championships, and in the process, we formed deep bonds of

friendship and support. This sense of camaraderie not only fueled our success on the field but also provided a safety net of encouragement and understanding that extended beyond the game. It taught me the invaluable lesson that we're stronger together, and that the support of others can be a powerful catalyst for personal growth and resilience.

3. **Pursue Your Passions:** Engaging in activities that bring you joy and fulfillment is essential for a happy life. Whether it's painting, writing, dancing, or spending time in nature, make time for the things that light you up. During my period of introspection, I discovered the profound impact that pursuing my passions had on my overall well-being. By exploring new hobbies and interests, such as experimenting with natural products, trying new recipes, and taking long walks in nature, I was able to reconnect with my authentic self and reignite my passion for life. These activities not only brought me joy and fulfillment but also served as a powerful antidote to the negative thought patterns that had once plagued me.

4. **Embrace Imperfection:** None of us are perfect, and that's okay. In fact, it's our imperfections that make us unique and beautiful. By embracing our flaws and accepting ourselves as we are, we release the burden of trying to be someone we're not and open ourselves up to greater joy and authenticity.

Cultivating happiness requires us to be intentional about our thoughts, our actions, and the company we keep. But the rewards are immeasurable. By embracing these practices and principles, we can create a life that is not only resilient but also overflowing with joy.

The Dawn of a Resilient Life

As we reach the end of this chapter, we stand on the precipice of a new beginning. The tools and insights we've gathered are more than just bandages for our wounds; they're the building blocks of a life that thrives in the face of adversity. We've learned that resilience isn't about avoiding setbacks but about embracing them as opportunities for growth. We've discovered that even in the darkest valleys, we can find a flicker of light that guides us toward healing and transformation.

The journey toward lasting happiness and contentment is far from over. It's a continuous dance between embracing our strengths and acknowledging our vulnerabilities. But armed with the knowledge and practices we've explored in this chapter, we're better equipped to navigate the twists and turns of life with grace and resilience. As we move into the final chapter, we'll take these lessons and weave them into the fabric of our daily lives, creating a tapestry of well-being that radiates from within. Remember, you're not alone in this journey. We're all travelers on this winding path, learning, growing, and evolving together. And as we continue to embrace our imperfections and celebrate our strengths, we'll discover that true happiness lies not in the absence of challenges, but in our ability to rise above them.

Chapter 7

Embracing a New Mindset for Life

We stand at the threshold of a new beginning, ready to weave the threads of healing and resilience we've gathered into the vibrant tapestry of our lives. This final chapter isn't about reaching some unattainable state of perfection or denying the existence of pain. It's about embracing the messy, beautiful, and ever-evolving nature of our human experience. It's about crafting a life that flourishes not in spite of our struggles, but because of them.

We'll delve into the art of integrating the tools and techniques we've learned into our daily routines, transforming them from fleeting moments of relief into the bedrock of a sustainable, joyful existence. We'll explore the power of self-care, nurturing our minds, bodies, and spirits with the same love and attention we would give to a cherished friend. And we'll dare to envision a future free from the shackles of our past, where happiness and contentment aren't fleeting emotions but a way of life.

This is our invitation to step into the dawn of a new era, one where we embrace our imperfections, celebrate our strengths, and create a life that's as unique and vibrant as we are.

Integrating All Techniques Into a Cohesive Lifestyle

The key to lasting change lies in integrating the techniques discussed throughout this book into your everyday life. This involves a commitment to routine practice, making meditation, mindfulness, and cognitive restructuring part of your daily routine, just as brushing your teeth or taking a shower has become habitual.

Habit formation is a powerful tool for transformation. By building new habits around positive thinking and healthy lifestyle choices, such as regular physical activity and balanced nutrition, you create a foundation for sustained well-being. Just as my high school basketball coach instilled in us the importance of consistent practice to achieve our goals on the court, so too must we practice these techniques consistently to achieve our goals of mental and emotional health.

Remember, this journey isn't a race but a marathon. There will be days when you feel energized and motivated, and there will be days when you stumble and fall. The key is to be kind to yourself, to embrace the process of continuous learning, and to adapt new strategies for mental and emotional health as you grow and your needs change.

Long-Term Strategies for Maintaining Mental Health and Emotional Well-Being

Sustaining mental health isn't a finish line you cross; it's about crafting a lifestyle that nourishes your mind, body, and spirit, a tapestry woven with threads of self-care, connection, and continuous learning.

Think of it as creating a blueprint for your well-being, a personalized map that guides you toward a life of balance and fulfillment. This blueprint includes:

☞ **Regular Mental Health Check-Ins:** Just as you schedule regular physical checkups to monitor your physical health, consider incorporating mental health evaluations into your routine. These check-ins can take various forms, from therapy sessions and coaching to heart-to-heart conversations with trusted friends or family members. The goal is to create a safe space where you can openly express your thoughts and feelings, gain valuable insights, and receive support on your journey.

☞ **Support Networks:** We're not meant to walk this path alone. Surround yourself with people who uplift and inspire you, who believe in your potential, and who celebrate your successes. Seek out friends who truly see you, hear you, and accept you for who you are, flaws and all. These relationships are the pillars of your support network, providing a haven where you can be vulnerable, share your struggles, and receive encouragement.

☞ **Lifelong Learning:** The journey of self-discovery is a continuous one. Never stop learning about mental health, emotional well-being, and the intricate connection between mind and body. Explore books, attend workshops, and engage in conversations that expand your understanding of yourself and the world around you. The more you learn, the more empowered you'll become to take charge of your health and create a life that's both fulfilling and joyful.

By weaving these practices into your daily life, you'll develop the resilience to weather life's storms, the wisdom to navigate its challenges, and the strength to create a future that's truly yours.

Inspiring a Vision for a Future Free From the Bondage of Suffering

With this blueprint in hand, it's time to dream big. Imagine a future where you're the architect of your own happiness, the master of your own destiny. Imagine a life where:

- ☞ **You Control Your Thoughts, Not the Other Way Around:** You have the tools and the power to actively manage your mental landscape, choosing thoughts that empower and uplift you.

- ☞ **Your Emotional Well-Being Is a Priority:** You treat your mental health with the same care and importance as your physical health, recognizing that they're interconnected and equally vital to your overall well-being.

- ☞ **Happiness and Contentment Are Within Reach:** You have developed the resilience and skills necessary to find joy and satisfaction in the everyday moments of your life.

This vision of a future free from suffering isn't just a fantasy; it's a tangible goal that can be achieved through intentional action and a shift in mindset.

I found myself in a similar situation, trapped in a codependent slump, believing that I needed someone else to help me write this very book. I sought help from a writer friend, but even after spending time with her, I couldn't produce any results. I even flew to Thailand, hoping that a friend there could guide me and unlock my creativity.

But what I truly discovered in Thailand was the freedom to simply be with myself. It was in those moments of solitude and introspection that I realized the power to write this book was already within me. No one else could extract my thoughts and translate them onto paper. It was up to me to harness my own creativity, love, and knowledge.

Once I embraced this realization, I was able to produce the results I had once thought were the responsibility of others. I realized that the love, support, and guidance I had been seeking externally were readily available within myself. It was a powerful lesson in self-reliance and the importance of trusting our own inner wisdom.

This experience is a testament to the power we have to create our own reality. By envisioning a future free from suffering and taking intentional steps to manifest that vision, we can break free from the chains of the past and embrace a life of greater peace, joy, and fulfillment. It's a reminder that we're not victims of our circumstances, but rather the architects of our own destiny.

Your Journey of Transformation

As we reach the end of our shared journey, I invite you to reflect on the profound transformation that has taken place within you. You've learned to navigate the treacherous waters of relapse, to tame your inner critic, and to embrace the healing power of forgiveness. You've discovered the alchemy of joy, transforming setbacks into stepping stones on the path to a more fulfilling life.

But the journey doesn't end here. It's an ongoing process of self-discovery, growth, and evolution. The tools and insights we've shared are merely a starting point, a foundation upon which you can build a life that's uniquely your own.

Remember, you're not alone in this endeavor. We're all travelers on this winding path, learning from one another, supporting each other through the storms, and celebrating each other's triumphs. As you continue to embrace your imperfections, cultivate gratitude, and nurture your passions, you'll discover that true happiness lies not in the absence of challenges, but in your ability to rise above them.

So, step boldly into the unknown, dear reader. Embrace the messy, beautiful journey that is life. May your path be filled with resilience, joy, and an unwavering belief in the power of your own transformation.

Conclusion

As we close this chapter of our shared journey, I extend a heartfelt invitation to you, dear reader. This book isn't just a collection of words on a page; it's a living testament to the transformative power of the human spirit and to the resilience that resides within each of us, waiting to be awakened.

I hope that this book has not only informed you but also ignited a spark within you; a spark of hope, a flicker of possibility. I hope it has shown you that even in the face of adversity, even when the weight of the world feels heavy on your shoulders, you have the power to choose a different path.

The tools and techniques we've explored together aren't mere Band-Aids for the wounds of life; they're a roadmap to a more fulfilling existence. They're the keys to unlocking the boundless potential that lies dormant within you, waiting to be unleashed.

But this book is just the beginning. The real magic happens when you take these tools and make them your own, weaving them into the fabric of your daily life. It's about embracing the journey of self-discovery, of continuously learning and growing, of becoming the best version of yourself.

So, I invite you to take what you've learned here and put it into practice. Experiment, explore, and discover what works best for you. Share your insights with others, and allow their wisdom to enrich your own journey.

Remember, you're not alone. We're all connected, all part of a vast tapestry of human experience. By supporting one another, by sharing our stories and our struggles, we create a collective wave of healing that can transform not only our own lives but also the world around us.

As you step into this new chapter of your life, may you carry with you the unwavering belief that you are capable of creating a truly extraordinary life; a life that's filled with joy, purpose, and unwavering resilience; a life that's a testament to the power of the human spirit to heal, to grow, and to thrive.

I would be honored if you would share your thoughts and experiences with this book. Your feedback is invaluable to me, as it helps me understand how my words have resonated with you and how I can continue to support you on your journey.

Have the tools and techniques shared in this book helped you in any way? Have you experienced any shifts in your mindset or your relationship with pain? What insights or practices have resonated with you the most?

By sharing your story, you not only help me grow as an author, but you also contribute to a community of healing and support. Your words may inspire others who are struggling, offering them hope and encouragement on their own paths to well-being.

So, please, take a moment to leave a review, share your thoughts on social media, or simply reach out. Your voice matters, and your story has the power to make a difference.

References

Apkarian, A. V., Bushnell, M. C., Treede, R.-D., & Zubieta, J.-K. (2005). Human brain mechanisms of pain perception and regulation in health and disease. *European Journal of Pain*, *9*(4), 463–463. https://doi.org/10.1016/j.ejpain.2004.11.0017

Buddha, G. (n.d.). *A quote by Gautama Buddha*. GoodReads. https://www.goodreads.com/quotes/6990654-what-you-think-you-become-what-you-feel-you-attract

Chopra, D. (2008). *The seven spiritual laws of success.* ReadHowYouWant.com.

Dailyinsightreport.com. (2023, July 25). *The benefits of incorporating meditation into your daily life.* Daily Insight Report. https://dailyinsightreport.com/the-benefits-of-incorporating-meditation-into-your-daily-life/

Dimidjian, S., Hollon, S. D., Dobson, K. S., Schmaling, K. B., Kohlenberg, R. J., Addis, M. E., Gallop, R., McGlinchey, J. B., Markley, D. K., Gollan, J. K., Atkins, D. C., Dunner, D. L., & Jacobson, N. S. (2006). Randomized trial of behavioral activation, cognitive therapy, and antidepressant medication in the acute treatment of adults with major depression. *Journal of Consulting and Clinical Psychology*, *74*(4), 658–670. https://doi.org/10.1037/0022-006X.74.4.658

Doidge, N. (2007, March 15). *The brain that changes itself: Stories of personal triumph from the frontiers of brain science.* Www.goodreads.com. https://www.goodreads.com/book/show/570172.The _Brain_that_Changes_Itself

Grossman, P., Niemann, L., Schmidt, S., & Walach, H. (2004, July 1). *Mindfulness-based stress reduction and health benefits. A meta-analysis.* Journal of Psychosomatic Research. https://pubmed.ncbi.nlm.nih.gov/15256293/

Hashmi, J. A., Baliki, M. N., Huang, L., Baria, A. T., Torbey, S., Hermann, K. M., Schnitzer, T. J., & Apkarian, A. V. (2013). Shape shifting pain: Chronification of back pain shifts brain representation from nociceptive to emotional circuits. *Brain, 136*(9), 2751–2768. https://doi.org/10.1093/brain/awt211

Hill, N. (2011, January 1). *Outwitting the devil: The secret to freedom and success* (S. L. Lechter, Ed.). Goodreads. https://www.goodreads.com/book/show/10713286-outwitting-the-devil

Jobs, S. (n.d.). *Steve Jobs quotes.* BrainyQuote. https://www.brainyquote.com/quotes/steve_jobs_41 6875

Kabat-Zinn, J. (1982). An outpatient program in behavioral medicine for chronic pain patients based on the practice of mindfulness meditation: Theoretical considerations and preliminary results. *General Hospital Psychiatry, 4*(1), 33–47. https://doi.org/10.1016/0163-8343(82)90026-3

Keng, S. L., Smoski, M. J., & Robins, C. J. (2011). Effects of mindfulness on psychological health: A review of empirical studies. *Clinical Psychology Review*, *31*(6), 1041–1056. https://doi.org/10.1016/j.cpr.2011.04.006

Killingsworth, M. A., & Gilbert, D. T. (2010). A wandering mind is an unhappy mind. *Science*, *330*(6006), 932–932. https://doi.org/10.1126/science.1192439

McEwen, B. S. (2008). Central effects of stress hormones in health and disease: Understanding the protective and damaging effects of stress and stress mediators. *European Journal of Pharmacology*, *583*(2-3), 174–185. https://doi.org/10.1016/j.ejphar.2007.11.071

Murphy, J. (2020). The power of your subconscious mind. In *Google Books*. https://books.google.com.uy/books?id=VYrTDwAAQBAJ&printsec=copyright&redir_esc=y#v=onepage&q&f=false

Nestler, E. J., Hyman, S., & Malenka, R. (2001, January 1). *Molecular neuropharmacology: A foundation for clinical neuroscience, second edition.* Goodreads. https://www.goodreads.com/book/show/2398583.Molecular_Neuropharmacology

Prater, M. (2018, August 17). *40 Jim Rohn quotes you'll never forget.* HubSpot.com. https://blog.hubspot.com/sales/jim-rohn-quotes

Rohn, J. (n.d.). *A quote by Jim Rohn.* GoodReads. https://www.goodreads.com/quotes/7898460-learn-to-work-harder-on-yourself-than-you-do-on

Singer, M. A. (n.d.). *Michael A. Singer quotes (author of The Untethered Soul).* GoodReads. https://www.goodreads.com/author/quotes/950132. Michael_A_Singer?page=27

Singer, M. A. (2007, October 3). *The untethered soul: The journey beyond yourself.* Goodreads. https://www.goodreads.com/book/show/1963638.Th e_Untethered_Soul

Tolle, E. (n.d.). *Eckhart Tolle quotes (author of The Power of Now).* GoodReads. https://www.goodreads.com/author/quotes/4493.Ec khart_Tolle

Tracey, I., & Mantyh, P. W. (2007). The cerebral signature for pain perception and its modulation. *Neuron, 55*(3), 377–391. https://doi.org/10.1016/j.neuron.2007.07.012

Tzu, L. (n.d.). *A quote by Lao Tzu.* GoodReads. https://www.goodreads.com/quotes/1339572-when-the-student-is-ready-the-teacher-will-appear-when

Walsch, N. D. (1995). *Conversations with god: An uncommon dialogue, book 1.* GoodReads. https://www.goodreads.com/book/show/15015.Conv ersations_with_God

Image References

Alexandra_Koch. (2021). *Image of success and the road* [Image]. Pixabay. https://pixabay.com/es/illustrations/%C3%A9xito-success-la-carretera-sendero-5964580/

CDD20. (2019). *Imagen de hombre, vacío y naturaleza* [Image]. *Pixabay.* https://pixabay.com/es/illustrations/hombre-vac%C3%ADo-alma-flores-franqueza-4052354/

Growtika. (2023). *An abstract image of a sphere with dots and lines* [Image]. Unsplash. https://unsplash.com/photos/an-abstract-image-of-a-sphere-with-dots-and-lines-nGoCBxiaRO0

Winstead, T. (2021a). *Flatlay photo of weekly planner* [Image]. Pexels. https://www.pexels.com/photo/flatlay-photo-of-weekly-planner-6690924/

Winstead, T. (2021b). *Illustration of a head and butterflies around the scalp and inside the brain* [Image]. Pexels. https://www.pexels.com/photo/illustration-of-a-head-and-butterflies-around-the-scalp-and-inside-the-brain-8849272/

www.ingramcontent.com/pod-product-compliance
Lightning Source LLC
Chambersburg PA
CBHW040155160726
48006CB00014B/1755